The Universal Postulate

HERBERT SPENCER

1853

TABLE OF CONTENTS

THE UNIVERSAL POSTULATE

HAVE we not cause to think that there exists some unestablished principle of reasoning-some principle which, though instinctively acted upon, is not entered amongst our logical canons? That men should have constructed so many systems of thought which we hold to be irrational, yet cannot satisfactorily refute, is strong ground for suspecting this. The possibility of defending theories so utterly at variance with universal belief as Idealism and Scepticism, and the doctrines of Fichte and Hegel, implies one of two things; either that there is some fundamental flaw in the modes of argument pursued, or that reason necessarily leads to unreasonable conclusions. Can there be any doubt which of these is the more probable? It is much easier to suppose that particular thinkings are incidentally fallacious, than that all thinking is essentially fallacious.

The fact that even in those who draw these incongruous inferences the intellect unceasingly protests against them, would alone be good ground for assuming that its laws have been broken. The "natural propensity," as Hume styles it, to take a realist view of things, is one which no man ever rid himself of by proving Realism logically false. When we remember that in all other cases valid deductions eventually become beliefs-that though erroneous preconceptions may for a time shut the door on them, yet increasing knowledge by and by reverses this proceeding-when we remember this, it seems more likely that the incredible deductions of metaphysicians should be vicious than that they should form the only exceptions.

Regard the philosopher objectively. Is it not clear that the faculties he is now employing in reasoning about consciousness and ideas are the same faculties with which in childhood he drew his simplest inferences? Must not the action of these faculties follow throughout, the same law? Must not the results of their action be therefore congruous? And when they are not congruous, does not the fact indicate something abnormal-some nonconformity with the laws of their action-some error, as we say?

Indeed, on looking at the matter in the abstract, the logical impossibility of these theories that conflict with universal belief becomes manifest. For clearly, unless we can transcend consciousness, all metaphysics can be nothing but an analysis of our knowledge by means of our knowledge-an inquiry by our intelligence into the decisions of our intelligence. We cannot carry on such an inquiry without taking for granted the trustworthiness of our intelligence. How then can we legitimately end in proving something at variance with our primary beliefs, and so proving our intelligence fundamentally untrustworthy? Intelligence cannot prove its own invalidity because it must postulate its own validity in doing this.

There seems ample ground, then, for thinking that some logical vice underlies the incredible conclusions which metaphysicians arrive at-a vice manifestly both deep-seated and prevalent; and one that is therefore worth seeking out with wider views than the refutation of the conclusions themselves.

§ 2. Certain, however, as seems the existence of some fallacy, a distinct identification of it has been found by no means easy. Right as Reid may have been in his conviction, he cannot be said to have demonstrated that he was so. His "Inquiry into the Human Mind" contains no disproof of Scepticism, but is little more than an elaborate protest against it. Whilst now and again raising the hope that he is about to expose some fundamental error in his opponent's argument, he constantly disappoints by ending with another emphatic condemnation of the conclusion it leads to. "An absurdity too gross to merit confutation"-"palpable absurdities" which "with the adepts pass for profound discoveries"-"to reason against any of these kinds of evidence (of the senses, memory, andc.) is absurd"-such are the expressions with which he commonly winds up a paragraph; expressions that fall harmlessly on the sceptic who admits the seeming ridiculousness of his inferences, but asks how they can be untrue if logically drawn. In his later work, the "Essays on the Intellectual Powers of Man," Reid still beats the air. He continues to assume all that Scepticism calls in question. In the chapter on "Principles taken for granted," he says:-"I perceive figure, colour, hardness, softness, motion, resistance, and such like things. But these are qualities, and must necessarily be in something that is figured, coloured, hard or soft, that moves or resists. .... We do not give the name of mind to thought, reason, or desire; but to that being which thinks, which reasons, which desires." Thus he adopts as premises what Hume rejects as conclusions. He finds no common ground on which he and the doubter alike stand, and standing on which they may try their strength; but having thrown down his gage, he remains outside the lists, and merely hurls at his opponent an occasional sarcasm. Regarded as contributions to psychology, his "Essays" have much merit; but as constituting an answer to Scepticism, they have none.

In the Dissertation appended to his edition of Reid's works, Sir William Hamilton places the Common-sense Philosophy on a more satisfactory footing. But though by the systematic coherence he gives to its doctrines, he makes it look more tenable, he does not render it criticism-proof. Unfortunately, some of his main positions are open to objection. Amongst the self-evident propositions with which he sets out, are these.

"Consciousness is to be presumed trustworthy until proved mendacious."

"The mendacity of consciousness is proved, if its data, immediately in themselves, or mediately in their necessary consequences, be shown to stand in mutual contradiction."

Now a sceptic might very properly argue that this test is worthless. For as the steps by which consciousness is to be proved mendacious are themselves states of consciousness, and as they must be assumed trustworthy in the act of proving that consciousness is not so, the process results in assuming the trustworthiness of particular states of consciousness, to prove the mendacity of consciousness in general. Or to apply the test specifically-Let it be shown that two data of consciousness stand in contradiction. Then consciousness is mendacious. But if consciousness is mendacious, then the consciousness of this contradiction is mendacious. Then consciousness is trustworthy. And so on for ever.

Doubtless this merely goes to show that the mendacity of consciousness cannot be proved; and does not therefore diminish its credibility. But it is nevertheless true, that the offer of a valueless guarantee lays open to cavil that which it is put forward to insure.

A much more serious objection, however, may be raised to the proposition, on which turns the whole defence of Common Sense versus Scepticism. Sir William Hamilton says:-"In the act of sensible perception I am conscious of two things;-of myself as the perceiving subject, and of an external reality in relation to my sense as the object perceived. * * * * each of these is apprehended equally and at once in the same indivisible energy;" or as he elsewhere phrases it-"in the same indivisible moment of intuition."

Now this alleged simultaneity in our consciousness of subject and object, on which Sir William Hamilton relies for his proof of Realism, will not only be disputed by many as not being uniformly confirmed by their experience, but there would be no sufficient warrant for his conclusions, did experience invariably endorse his premiss. At a future stage of the argument, we propose to adduce evidence countenancing the belief, that in the act of perception our consciousness of subject and object is not simultaneous; but even were there no such evidence, this apparent simultaneity would be inadequate proof of real simultaneity.

For it must be remembered, that states of consciousness which originally occurred in distinct succession do by constant association come to follow one another so rapidly as to seem inseparable; and that in virtue of this law we ultimately unite a whole group of perceptions so instantaneously, that they appear as one perception. On looking at a book, we seem to take in all its leading properties "in the same indivisible energy." We cannot detect any lapse of time between our recognition of the book as a whole and our recognition of the parts we see: yet it is universally admitted, that the unseen sides of the book are inferred from the seen sides. We cannot detect any lapse of time between our recognition of the solidity of the book and our recognition of its colour and extension: yet it is universally admitted, that the solidity is inferred from these. And as all inferred ideas must come after those from which they are inferred, it is clear that we do not recognise the various properties of the book simultaneously, though we seem to do so. Were apparent simultaneity in the acts of consciousness a proof of real simultaneity, nothing would be clearer than that we perceive an object and its distance from us "in the same indivisible moment of intuition;" for it is impossible to distinguish any interval between these perceptions. Yet no fact in psychology is better established than this,-that the perception of a thing's distance is subsequent to the perception of the thing itself-is a deduction from the mode in which the thing affects us; and that the apparent simultaneity is in truth a succession too rapid for detection.

Hence, as there is no obvious reason why the apparent simultaneity in our consciousness of subject and object may not be of like nature, the position that subject and object are apprehended "in the same indivisible moment of intuition," cannot be considered unquestionable; and is consequently not a fit basis for a refutation of Scepticism. Some other first principle must be found.

§ 3. When we try to reduce the genesis of our knowledge to scientific ordination, and when to this end we search for the fundamental fact-the fact on which all knowledge depends, we meet the difficulty that there are several facts apparently answering to this description. Personal existence, the existence of ideas, of consciousness, of beliefs-these look equally primordial. Each seems to pre-suppose one or more of the others; and yet each in turn may be assigned with some plausibility as the basis of the others. Personal existence may be held the most certain fact of all. Yet it may be argued, that personal existence is merely a belief; and that the existence of beliefs is, therefore, more certain than personal existence. To which again there is the reply that a belief implies something believed; and that this something believed must be antecedent to, and more certain than, the belief. All things are resolvable into ideas, is another position for which much may be said. But this position is liable to the criticism that ideas presuppose something to take cognizance of them-a consciousness; and that all ideas being states of consciousness, the existence of consciousness must be prior to the existence of ideas. In rejoinder to which it is urged, that we become conscious only by the reception of ideas; and hence that there must be an idea before there can be consciousness. If it be said that ideas and consciousness must be classed amongst beliefs-that we have no other proof of their existence than that we believe them to exist-there comes the answer that beliefs are themselves ideas or states of consciousness; and this again may be met by saying that the conclusion that beliefs are states of consciousness is itself a belief. Thus we are driven from one position to another, only that we may relinquish that for a third; until there appears no alternative but to assume these facts to be equally fundamental-to lie on the same plane; either as mutually dependent facts, or as different aspects of the same fact.

On carefully reconsidering the matter, however, we may perceive that be the genesis of these facts simultaneous or successive, and if successive whatever be the order, there is still one of them which being unavoidably taken for granted, in every process of thought, must necessarily have priority of the others; namely, belief. Every logical act of the intellect is a predication-is an assertion that something is; and this is what we call belief. Each major premiss is a belief; each minor premiss is a belief; each conclusion is a belief. An argument is a series of dependent beliefs. Hence all connected thought being made up of beliefs, it is clear that be the propositions it embodies what they may-be they even the existence of consciousness, of ideas, of personality-they must be less certain than the existence of beliefs.

Or to state the matter in another form-Belief is the recognition of existence-is a knowing of the existent from the non-existent. All our reasoning is a distinguishing of truth from error-of that which exists from that which does not. Consequently upon the reality of the distinction we make between that which is, and that which is not; or, in other words-on the reality of belief depends the possibility of reasoning. We may deny all other things and yet leave our logical forms intact. But deny beliefs and not only do the things about which we argue disappear; argument itself disappears. Now the thing which being abolished carries everything else with it must be the fundamental thing.

It may seem very clear that in order of genesis, belief is not primary but secondary. It may be plausibly urged that it is a particular state of the ego, and must therefore exist subsequently to the ego; or that it is a complex idea, dependent upon, and arising out of, simple ideas; or that it is not an idea at all, but a peculiarity in certain of our ideas. But cogent as may be the arguments brought in support of these propositions, they cannot touch the conclusion above drawn. For each of these propositions is itself a belief; and each of the reasons given in proof of it is a belief. Dig down as deep as we may, we can never get to anything more fundamental; seeing that the deepest thing we reach becomes a belief at the moment of its disclosure, and for logical purposes can never be anything else. Let it be granted, for argument's sake, that all our beliefs are predications concerning pre-existing things-sensations, ideas, consciousness; let it be granted that until these exist there can be no predications about them-no beliefs; let it be granted, that in reasoning, or in forming beliefs, we, as it were, look down upon and inspect these sensations and ideas, and observe certain of their properties, which we could not do unless they were previously there-let all this be granted; it nevertheless remains true, that as the reasoning faculty can deal with no facts until they are cognized by it-as until they are cognized by it they are to it non-existent-it follows that in being cognized, that is, in becoming beliefs, they begin to exist relatively to our reason. Whether really pre-existent or not they can have no logical pre-existence; since the being perceived to exist is the being believed.

Hence belief is the fact which, to our intellects, is antecedent to, and inclusive of, all other facts. It is the form in which every fact must present itself to us, and therefore underlies every fact. It alone of all things cannot be denied without direct self-contradiction. The propositions-there is no consciousness, there are no ideas, there is no personal identity, may be absurd; but they are not immediately self-destructive. To say, however, there is no belief, is to utter a belief which denies itself-is to draw a distinction between that which is, and that which is not, and at the same time to say that we do not distinguish between that which is, and that which is not.

Belief, then, being the ultimate fact which we can never transcend, there next come the questions-How do we class our beliefs? Why do we consider certain of our beliefs more trustworthy than others? What is the peculiarity of those beliefs which we never question, and to which all the rest of our beliefs defer?

To give any psychological answer-to discuss Hume's theory of belief or any other, would be beside the argument. No concrete analysis of belief is possible without taking for granted ideas, or consciousness, or personal identity; and to do this would be to involve in our desired test of credibility the very theories it is proposed to test by it. At present our assumptions are limited to three-existence, its correlative non-existence, and a cognition of the difference, that is-belief. The problem is to find a canon of belief without assuming anything further. For if in classing our beliefs according to their degrees of validity, some fourth thing should be taken for granted, the existence of such degrees of validity could have no greater certainty than the existence of this fourth thing.

Existence, non-existence, and belief, being thus the terms to which we are confined, there is clearly no alternative but to distinguish amongst our beliefs by qualities expressible in the other two terms. At first sight this appears hopeless; for whilst there can be existent beliefs, there cannot be non-existent beliefs. But though it seems paradoxical to say so, we may, by the union of the two terms existence and non-existence, obtain a third which describes the nature of some of our beliefs as contrasted with others. Here at least is the only possible classification-that into beliefs of which existence alone can be predicated, and beliefs of which partly existence and partly non-existence can be predicated-beliefs that invariably exist, and beliefs that do not invariably exist. That this division really corresponds with our experience scarcely needs saying. All know that, on the one hand, they have beliefs which are constant and which no mental effort can for a moment rid them of; whilst on the other they have beliefs which are not only changed by evidence but which can be temporarily suppressed by the imagination.

To say that as a corollary from this, the invariable existence of a belief is our final test of certainty-to say that where there are conflicting propositions, one of which corresponds to an invariably existent belief whilst the other does not, we must adopt the one that so corresponds, is needless-is in fact a truism. For an invariably existent belief is, by virtue of its being one, incapable of being replaced by any other. It is not that we ought to adopt that belief, but that we can do nothing else. In saying that it is invariably existent we say that there is no alternative belief.

That its invariable existence is the ultimate guarantee assignable for any belief, is indeed a conclusion which may be otherwise arrived at. For when we assign for any belief, a deeper belief on which it rests-when as warrant for some belief A, we cite some fundamental belief B which involves it, and say that we hold the belief A because it is implied in the belief B, it is manifest that the validity of the warrant depends upon the validity of the belief that B does involve A; and for this belief we have no other reason to assign but that it exists. So that supposing we knew the belief B to possess absolute truth, it could never give to the consequent belief A any higher guarantee than this of invariable existence; seeing that we can produce no higher guarantee for our belief that the one involves the other.

Or perhaps the fact may be more clearly shown thus:-If we assign as a reason for any belief the belief on which it rests, and then assign for that belief an anterior one, and so on continuously, it is clear that we must eventually come to the end of the series-must arrive at some primordial belief of which no proof can be given. This remains true, whatever theory we hold respecting the origin of our knowledge. For if we say that all knowledge is organized experience, and that, in assigning one belief in proof of another, we are simply assigning a wider experience in proof of a narrower, it is clear that we cannot continue to assign wider and wider experiences in proof of each other, without arriving finally at the widest. As our experience had a beginning, it follows that, in tracing it backwards, we must ultimately come to our first or deepest experience-an experience which has no other to rest upon. Similarly with the hypothesis of fundamental ideas. An analytical examination of beliefs must eventually bring us down to these; and for these the hypothesis itself implies that no reason is assignable. Hence, whether our lowest beliefs be innate or derived from experience, it is equally clear that, as they do not admit of proof, we can but say that they invariably exist. And whilst this fact of their invariable existence is alone our warrant for them, it at the same time expresses the necessity we are under of holding them.

It results, then, from all that has been said,-first, that the existence of beliefs is the fundamental fact; and second, that beliefs which invariably exist are those which, both rationally and of necessity, we must adopt.

§ 4. The controversy that has lately been carried on respecting the nature and origin of necessary truths presents a fit field for initiating this doctrine.

In his "Philosophy of the Inductive Sciences," Dr. Whewell defines necessary truths as "those in which we not only learn that the proposition is true, but see that it must be true; in which the negation of the truth is not only false, but impossible; in which we cannot, even by an effort of imagination, or in a supposition, conceive the reverse of that which is asserted." Or, to quote the abridged form to which Mr. Mill, in his criticism, reduces it-"A necessary truth is a proposition the negation of which is not only false but inconceivable."

The first thing to be said of this definition is, that it includes many other truths than those called "necessary." His personal existence is a truth which every man can cite this warrant for. To his consciousness it is a truth of which the negation is inconceivable. That he might not exist he can conceive well enough; but that he does not exist he finds it impossible to conceive. The pain felt on plunging the hand into scalding water, is a pain which the sufferer cannot, "by an effort of imagination," conceive non-existent. Were the existence of the pain a truth of which the negation was conceivable, he would quickly conceive the negation, and thus rid himself of the pain. But so convenient a mode of obtaining relief, the sufferer finds, to his cost, impracticable. Unless, therefore, the propositions-"I exist," "I feel pain," and others like them, be classed as necessary truths, the definition will not hold. Doubtless there is a wide difference between the universal truths which Dr. Whewell has in view, and the particular truths here instanced; but the difference is not that implied in his definition.

This fact, that the truths of immediate perception have the same warrant as the so-called necessary truths, is quite in harmony with, and, indeed, serves to confirm, the arguments which Mr. Mill brings forward to disprove the alleged à priori character of these necessary truths. But whilst quite agreeing with him in the belief that axioms are simply "our earliest inductions from experience," it is possible to differ from him widely as to the worth of the test of inconceivableness. In attacking the theory we think he has needlessly undervalued the witness. He says:-

"I cannot but wonder that so much stress should be laid on the circumstance of inconceivableness, when there is ample experience to show that our capacity or incapacity of conceiving a thing has very little to do with the possibility of the thing in itself; but is, in truth, very much an affair of accident, and depends on the past history and habits of our own minds. .... When we have often seen and thought of two things together, and have never, in any one instance, either seen or thought of them separately, there is, by the primary law of association, an increasing difficulty, which may, in the end, become insuperable, if conceiving the two things apart. .... There are remarkable instances of this in the history of science: instances in which the most instructed men rejected as impossible, because inconceivable, things which their posterity, by earlier practice and longer perseverance in the attempt, found it quite easy to conceive, and which everybody now knows to be true."-"System of Logic," pp. 265, 266.

And he then proceeds to give sundry illustrations showing this dependence of conceivability upon experience-illustrations, however, which, as will hereafter be shown, are not altogether unobjectionable.

Granting, nevertheless, that the evidence assigned affords sufficient disproof of the doctrine that truths of which the negation is inconceivable are à priori, it does not really warrant Mr. Mill's inference that it is absurd "to reject a proposition as impossible on no other ground than its inconceivableness;" however much it may seem to warrant him. For the facts cited simply go to show that men have mistaken for inconceivable things, some things which were not inconceivable-a species of error which, if it vitiates the test of inconceivableness, must similarly vitiate all tests whatever. We consider an inference logically drawn from an established premiss to be true. Yet, in millions of cases, men have been wrong in the inferences they have thought thus drawn. Do we, therefore, argue that it is absurd to consider an inference true "on no other ground" than that it is logically drawn from an established premiss? No; we say that though men may have taken for logical inferences, inferences that were not logical, there nevertheless are logical inferences, and that we are justified in assuming the truth of what seem to us such, until better instructed. Similarly, though men may have thought some things inconceivable which were not so, there may still be inconceivable things; and the inability to conceive the negation of a thing, may still be our best warrant for believing it.

Granting the entire truth of Mr. Mill's position, that, during any phase of human progress, the ability or inability to form a specific conception wholly depends on the experiences men have had; and that, by a widening of their experiences, they may, by and by, be enabled to conceive things before inconceivable to them; it may still be argued that as, at any time, the best warrant men can have for a belief is the perfect agreement of all pre-existing experience in support of it, it follows that, at any time, the inconceivableness of its negation is the deepest test any belief admits of. Though occasionally it may prove an imperfect test, yet as our most certain beliefs are capable of no better, to doubt any one belief because we have no higher guarantee for it is really to doubt all beliefs.

Or to state the case in another form-If all our knowledge is derived from experience, then our notions of possible and impossible are derived from experience. Possible means-not at variance with our experience; impossible means-wholly at variance with our experience. Clearly, unless we possess fundamental ideas, or can gain a knowledge of things in themselves, no logical process can give to the notion, impossible, any larger meaning than this. But if, at any time, the inability of men to conceive the negation of a given proposition simply proves that their experience, up to that time, has, without exception, confirmed such proposition; then when they assert that its untruth is impossible, they really assert no more than when they assert that its negation is inconceivable. If, subsequently, it turn out that the proposition is untrue; and if it be therefore argued that men should not have held its untruth impossible because inconceivable, we reply, that to say this is to condemn the use of the word impossible altogether. If the inconceivability of a thing be considered insufficient warrant for asserting its impossibility, it is implied that there can exist a sufficient warrant; but such warrant, whatever its kind, must be originally derived from experience; and if further experience may invalidate the warrant of inconceivableness, further experience may invalidate any warrant on which we assert impossibility. Therefore, we should call nothing impossible.

It is, indeed, surprising that so acute a critic as Mr. Mill should not have seen that his own analysis supplies the best justification of this test of inconceivableness. What is the object of any such test? To insure a correspondence between subjective beliefs and objective facts. Well, objective facts are ever impressing themselves upon us; our experience is a register of these objective facts; and the inconceivableness of a thing implies that it is wholly at variance with the register. Even were this all, it is not clear how, if every truth is primarily inductive, any better test of truth could exist. But it must be remembered that whilst many of these facts, impressing themselves upon us, are occasional; whilst others again are very general; some are universal and unchanging. These universal and unchanging facts are, by the hypothesis, certain to establish beliefs of which the negations are inconceivable; whilst the others are not certain to do this, and if they do, subsequent facts will reverse their action. Hence if, after an immense accumulation of experiences, there remain beliefs of which the negation is still inconceivable, most, if not all of them, must correspond to universal objective facts. If there be, as Mr. Mill holds, certain absolute uniformities in nature; if these uniformities produce, as they must, absolute uniformities in our experience; and if, as he shows, these absolute uniformities in our experience disable us from conceiving the negations of them; then answering to each absolute uniformity in nature which we can cognize, there must exist in us a belief of which the negation is inconceivable, and which is absolutely true. In this wide range of cases subjective inconceivableness must correspond to objective impossibility. Further experience will produce correspondence where it may not yet exist; and we may expect the correspondence to become ultimately complete. In nearly all cases this test of inconceivableness must be valid now; and where it is not, it still expresses the net result of our experience thus far; which is the most that any test can do.

But the inconsistency into which Mr. Mill has here fallen, is most clearly seen in the second of his two chapters on "Demonstration and Necessary Truths."

He admits in this, the validity of proof by a reductio ad absurdum. But what is a reductio ad absurdum unless a reduction to inconceivableness? And why, if inconceivableness be in other cases an insufficient ground for rejecting a proposition as impossible, is it a sufficient ground in this case?

Again, calling in question the necessity commonly ascribed to the deductive sciences, he says:-

"The results of these sciences are indeed necessary, in the sense of necessarily following from certain first principles, called axioms and definitions; of being certainly true, if these axioms and definitions are so. But their claim to the character of necessity in any sense beyond this .... must depend on the previous establishment of such a claim in favour of the definitions and axioms themselves."-Chapter vi.

Or, as he previously expresses the same view:-

"The only sense in which necessity can be ascribed to the conclusions of any scientific investigation, is that of necessarily following from some assumption which, by the conditions of the inquiry, is not to be questioned."-Chapter v.

Here, and throughout the whole of his argument, Mr. Mill assumes that there is something more certain in a demonstration than in anything else-some necessary truth in the steps of our reasoning, which is not possessed by the axioms they start from. How can this assumption be justified? In each successive syllogism the dependence of the conclusion upon its premisses is a truth of which we have no other proof than the inconceivability of the negation. Unless our perception of logical truth is à priori, which Mr. Mill will not contend, it too, like our perceptions of mathematical truth, has been gained from experience. In the one case, as in the other, we have simply an induction, with which no fact has, to our knowledge, ever conflicted. And if this be an insufficient warrant for asserting the necessity of the one order of truth, it is an insufficient warrant for asserting the necessity of the other.

How complete is the parallelism may indeed be best proved from Mr. Mill's own admissions. In an earlier chapter he has very clearly shown that by analysis of the syllogism we arrive at "a fundamental principle, or rather two principles, strikingly resembling the axioms of mathematics. The first, which is the principle of affirmative syllogisms, is, that things which coexist with the same thing, coexist with one another. The second is the principle of negative syllogisms, and is to this effect: that a thing which coexists with another thing, with which other a third thing does not coexist, is not coexistent with that third thing." Elsewhere, if we remember rightly, he points out the remarkable analogy between this logical axiom-things which coexist with the same thing, coexist with one another-and the mathematical axiom-things which are equal to the same thing are equal to one another. Analogous, however, as they are, and similarly derived as they must be, Mr. Mill claims for the first a necessity which he denies to the last. When, as above, he asserts that the deductive sciences are not necessary, save "in the sense of necessarily following from certain first principles called axioms and definitions, of being certainly true if those axioms and definitions are so"-he assumes that whilst the mathematical axioms possess only hypothetical truth, this logical axiom involved in every step of the demonstration possesses absolute truth-that whilst the inconceivability of its negation is an imperfect guarantee for the one, it is a perfect guarantee for the other. Evidently this is an untenable position. Unless it can be shown that this truth-things which coexist with the same thing coexist with each other-has some higher warrant than the inconceivability of its negation, (which cannot be shown,) it must be admitted that axioms and demonstration stand on the same footing, and that if necessity be denied to the one, it must be denied to the other; and, indeed, to all things whatever.

Of objections to the test of inconceivability it remains only to notice the one pointed out by Sir William Hamilton in his edition of Reid (p. 377). In proof that inconceivability is not a criterion of impossibility, he cites the fact, that "we can neither conceive, on the one hand, an ultimate minimum of space or time; nor can we, on the other, conceive their infinite divisibility. In like manner, we cannot conceive the absolute commencement of time, nor the utmost limit of space, and are yet equally unable to conceive them without any commencement or limit." The implication being, that as there must be either minimum or no minimum, limit or no limit, one of the two inconceivable things must in each case be true. Exception might be taken to this argument on several grounds; on the ground that space and time are not strictly conceivable things at all in the sense that other things are; on the ground that the alleged inconceivableness of a minimum or a limit is not really of the same nature as those with which it is classed-is not due to an arrest of the conceptive power, but a baffling of it-is not an inability to get rid of a certain conception, but an inability to form any conception. Moreover, it might be urged that there is no true parallelism between these cases in which both alternatives are alike inconceivable, and all other cases, in which one alternative is conceivable and the other not. Passing over these points, however, and granting, as has already been granted, that conceivableness depends on experience, and that hence, in respect to all things beyond the measure of our faculties it must ever remain an inapplicable test-granting all this, we say, Sir William Hamilton's argument may still be met. He says that inconceivability is no criterion of impossibility. Why? Because, of two propositions, one of which must be true, it proves both impossible-it proves that space cannot have a limit, because a limit is inconceivable, and yet that it must have a limit, because unlimited space is inconceivable; it proves, therefore, that space has a limit and has no limit, which is absurd. How absurd? Absurd, because "it is impossible for the same thing to be and not to be." But how do we know that it is impossible for the same thing to be and not to be? what is our criterion of this impossibility? Can Sir William Hamilton assign any other than this same inconceivability? If not, his argument is self-destructive; seeing that he assumes the validity of the test in proving its invalidity.

§ 5. A right comprehension of this matter will now, however, be readily arrived at on recalling the propositions awhile since established; namely, that the existence of beliefs is the fundamental fact, and that beliefs which invariably exist are those which both rationally and of necessity we must adopt. For when, to the fact that the invariable existence of a belief is the deepest warrant we can have for it, we add the further fact that we consider those beliefs true of which the negations are inconceivable, it becomes at once obvious that the inconceivability of its negation is the test by which we ascertain whether a given belief invariably exists or not.

Instinctively we recognise the truth above demonstrated, that its invariable existence is the ultimate authority for any belief; or rather, we yield to the rigorous necessity of holding any belief that does invariably exist: the fact that it invariably exists being the obverse of the fact that there is no alternative belief. But how do we ascertain that a given belief is invariably existent-that we have no alternative belief? Evidently we can do this only by trying to make such belief non-existent-by trying to put some other belief in its place; or, in other words-by trying to conceive the negation of it. When, failing by any mental effort to make it disappear, even for a moment, we say that nothing else is conceivable, and that it is therefore unquestionably true, we practically say that it is true because it is a belief which invariably exists.

What we mean by this word, true-whether we express by it an assumed correspondence between some objective fact and our subjective state, or whether it really implies nothing more than the continued existence of the belief to which it is applied, it would be out of place here to inquire. At present we have to consider the contents of the intellect solely as a system of beliefs, with a view to determine their relative validity. We have seen that beliefs must be their own sureties-that an indestructible belief can have no other warrant than its indestructibility; and what we have just found is, that the inconceivableness of its negation is simply an experimental proof of its indestructibility.

It results then that for our primary beliefs, the fact of invariable existence tested by an abortive effort to cause non-existence, is the only reason assignable. If in justifying those of our beliefs which rest upon other beliefs we must ultimately come down to this as the foundation of the series, it follows that all beliefs not based upon other beliefs must rest directly on this foundation. Such we find to be the case. The truths of immediate consciousness have no other warrant. For the proposition "I am," no one who utters it can find any proof but the invariable existence of his belief in it. And that he cannot for an instant displace this belief by any other-cannot conceive otherwise-is the only proof he can give of its invariable existence. So, too, is it with sensations. When cold, we cannot get rid of our belief in the feeling of coldness as long as that feeling continues-cannot while cold conceive that we are warm. Such belief, though not invariably existent in an absolute sense, is so in a relative one: it exists as long as the sensation exists. Whilst the proposition remains true, the negation of it remains inconceivable. Hence, properly understood, the belief in a sensation has the same warrant as belief in personal existence. In each case the belief invariably exists whilst its subject-matter exists-in the sensation whilst the sensation continues, in personal existence whilst personal existence continues.

And here we may recognise the real distinction between those universal truths which Dr. Whewell has supposed to stand alone in the inconceivableness of their negations, and those particular truths which we find to have the same guarantee. It is in the prevalence of the subject-matter that the difference consists. Whilst looking at the sun a man can no more conceive that he is then looking into darkness, than he can conceive the part greater than the whole. How then does the belief-this is sun-light, differ in nature from the belief-the whole is greater than its part? Simply thus; that in the one instance the antecedents of the conviction are present only on special occasions, whilst in the other they are present on all occasions. In either case subject the mind to the required antecedents, and no belief save the appropriate one is conceivable. But whilst in the first case only a single object serves for antecedent, in the other any object, real or imagined, serves for antecedent.

Not only, however, is the invariable existence of a belief our sole warrant for every truth of immediate consciousness, and for every primary generalization of the truths of immediate consciousness-every axiom, but it is our sole warrant for every demonstration. Logic is simply a systematization of the process by which we indirectly obtain this warrant for beliefs that do not directly possess it. To gain the strongest conviction possible respecting any complex fact, we either analytically descend from it by successive steps, each of which we unconsciously test by the inconceivableness of its negation, until we reach some axiom or truth which we have similarly tested, or we synthetically ascend from such axiom or truth by such steps. In either case we connect some isolated belief, with a belief which invariably exists, by a series of intermediate beliefs which invariably exist.

To prevent misapprehension on the part of those who have not much considered the matter, it may be well, as we have yet spoken only of beliefs which invariably exist, to contrast them with a belief which, though strong, does not invariably exist; especially as in doing this we shall have an opportunity of clearing up the seeming confusion which some may have perceived in the last few pages between beliefs and conceptions-a seeming confusion which the abstract nature of the argument has hitherto forbidden us to notice.

We commonly regard the belief that the sun will rise to-morrow as a constant one. It may, however, for an interval be destroyed. We find that by an effort of imagination, as we call it, the sun may be supposed to explode, burn out, or in some way be prevented from appearing to-morrow; and during the time in which we are figuring to ourselves the non-appearance of the sun to-morrow, the belief that he will appear is non-existent. It is very true that this belief is quickly reproduced; but it is none the less true that it is temporarily annihilated. Possibly, indeed, it may be alleged that the belief is never really absent, but that it remains even whilst we are conceiving the event to be otherwise. This, however, is an illusion consequent upon our habit of using words without fully realizing their meanings, and so mistaking verbal propositions for real ones. On taking care that our thoughts duly respond to the expressions, we shall find that the belief in the sun's rising to-morrow consists in a mental representation of the occurrence of certain phenomena at a certain time. And if so, it is clear that we cannot conceive the event otherwise-cannot represent to ourselves the non-occurrence of the phenomena, without abolishing the representation of their occurrence; that is,-without abolishing the belief. Though in common language we speak of a belief as something separate from the conception to which it relates, yet on analysis we find that we simply express by it a certain property of such conception-its persistence. When after given antecedents there arises a state of consciousness which we can change with very little effort, we have a weak belief; when the state of consciousness is one which we can change with difficulty, we call the belief a strong one; when it is one which we find ourselves utterly unable to change, we consider it a belief of the highest order. As then in each of these classes the belief is not a something more than the state of consciousness, but merely expresses its persistence, it follows that in no case can the state of consciousness be changed, even temporarily, without the belief becoming non-existent for a corresponding period. The belief being the persistence, the persistence cannot be destroyed without the belief being destroyed. And hence the rationale of testing the invariable existence of a belief in a given proposition by the inconceivableness of its negation; seeing that the effort to conceive the negation of the proposition is the effort to change the state of consciousness which arises after certain antecedents; and could this be done-could the persistence of the state of consciousness be broken-the belief would be proved to be not invariably existent.[1]

Dismissing, however, all psychological explanations, which are allowable here only as being needed to meet a psychological objection, and returning to the purely abstract view of the matter, we see-first, that belief is fundamental, and that the invariable existence of a belief is our highest warrant for it; second, that we can ascertain the invariable existence of a belief only as we ascertain the invariable existence of anything else, by observing whether under any circumstances it is absent from the place in which it occurs; third, that the effort to conceive the negation of a belief is the looking in the place in which it occurs, (viz., after its antecedents,) and observing whether there are any occasions on which it is absent, or can be made absent; and fourth, that when we fail to find such occasions-when we perceive that the negation of the belief is inconceivable-we have all possible warrant for asserting the invariability of its existence; and, in asserting this, we express alike our logical justification of it, and the inexorable necessity we are under of holding it. Mean what we may by the word truth, we have no choice but to hold that a belief which is proved, by the inconceivableness of its negation, to invariably exist, is true. We have seen that this is the assumption on which every conclusion whatever ultimately rests. We have no other guarantee for the reality of consciousness, of sensations, of personal existence; we have no other guarantee for any axiom; we have no other guarantee for any step in a demonstration. Hence, as being taken for granted in every act of the understanding, it must be regarded as the Universal Postulate.

§ 6. An appeal to this Universal Postulate as an absolute warrant for any conviction may still, however, be objected to, on the ground that as it has on past occasions proved an insufficient warrant, it may prove so again. Beliefs that once were shown by the inconceivableness of their negations to invariably exist, have since been found untrue. And as beliefs that now possess this character may some day share the same fate, the test is clearly not an infallible one.

There is, doubtless, force in this argument, though not so much as at first appears. As we hinted when commenting on his position, the evidence cited by Mr. Mill, to show that inconceivable things may yet be true, is not strictly applicable evidence. There is a wide difference in nature between the cases in which the test has been found fallacious, and those in which we may regard it as trustworthy-a difference arising from the relative complexities of the conceptions involved. When, on receiving a sensation, the subject of it finding himself unable to conceive that he is not receiving it, asserts that he is receiving it, it is clear that he deals only with one state of consciousness of which he simply recognises the continued existence. On the other hand, those Greek philosophers referred to by Mr. Mill, who "could not credit the existence of antipodes," who "were unable to conceive, in opposition to old association, the force of gravity acting upwards instead of downwards," and who, therefore, denied that there could be men on the other side of the earth-were dealing with many states of consciousness and with the connexions between them. There entered into their proposition the concepts, Earth, man, distance, position, force, and the various relations of these to each other. Evidently, then, these cases differ so widely, that what may be a legitimate test in the first, may be an illegitimate one in the second. We must distinguish between those appeals to the Universal Postulate in which the act of thought is decomposable, and those in which it is undecomposable. In proportion as the number of concepts which a proposition involves is great, and the mental transitions from concept to concept are numerous, the fallibility of the test will increase; and will do this because the formation of the belief is separable into many steps, each of which involves the postulate.

And here, indeed, we get hold of the clue which leads us out of this logical maze. Let it be granted, that a belief which invariably exists, though the most certain possible to us, is yet, not necessarily true. Let it be granted, that either from insufficient experience, or from non-agreement between the subjective and the objective, the inconceivable and the impossible may not correspond even within our mental range. Let it be granted, that for the validity even of a single undecomposable act of thought, the Universal Postulate is an imperfect warrant. Let all this, we say, be granted. Still, be the test fallible or not, the probability of error in any inference will increase in proportion to the number of times the truth of the test has been assumed in arriving at it. If the postulate be uniformly valid, it must yet happen, that as we are liable to mental lapsus, we shall occasionally think we have its warrant when we have not; and in each case the chances of our having done this will vary directly as the number of times we have claimed its warrant. If the postulate be not uniformly valid, then a further source of error is introduced, the effects of which vary in the same ratio. Hence, on either supposition, it follows that that must be the most certain conclusion, at which, starting from the postulate itself, we arrive by the fewest assumptions of the postulate.

We instinctively recognise this fact in our ordinary modes of proof. We hold it more certain that 2 and 2 make 4, than that $5 + 7 + 6 + 9 + 8$ make 35. We find that every fresh assumption of the postulate involves some risk of error; and, indeed, where the calculation is extremely intricate, and the assumptions therefore extremely numerous, our experience teaches us that the probability that there has been a wrong assumption is greater than the probability that there has not. So too in argument. We lose faith in a long series of steps, however logical they may seem, unless we can test the inference by appeal to fact-that is, unless we can get at the inference by a single use of the postulate.

Do we not here then discern a rigorous test of the relative validity of conflicting conclusions? Not only as judged instinctively, but as judged by a fundamental logic, that must be the most certain conclusion which involves the postulate the fewest times. We find that under any circumstances-whether the postulate be uniformly true or not, this must hold good. Here, therefore, we have a method of ascertaining the respective values of all inferences.

Let us by the help of this method examine some of the leading systems of philosophy.

§ 7. The Idealism of Berkeley, in common with all kindred systems of thought, is obviously, when regarded from our present stand-point, open to the criticism that it consists of a series of propositions, no one of which possesses greater certainty than the single proposition which it sets out to disprove. Not to rest in this general statement of the objection, however, let us consider its application in detail.

It is an awkward fact, that Idealism cannot state its case without assuming Realism by the way. Erase from its argument all terms implying the objective reality of things, and its argument falls to pieces. Instance in illustration of this a passage from the first of Berkeley's Dialogues.

"Philonous. Then, as to sounds, what must we think of them? Are they accidents really inherent in external bodies, or not?

"Hylas. That they inhere not in the sonorous bodies, is plain from hence; because a bell, struck in the exhausted receiver of an air-pump, sends forth no sound. The air, therefore, must be thought the subject of sound.

"Phil. What reason is there for that, Hylas?

"Hyl. Because, when any motion is raised in the air, we perceive a sound, greater or lesser, in proportion to the air's motion; but, without some motion in the air, we never hear any sound at all.

"Phil. And granting that we never hear a sound but when some motion is produced in the air, yet I do not see how you can infer, from thence, that the sound itself is in the air."

If now we demur to the many obvious assumptions of Realism which this reasoning involves, and insist on Berkeley re-stating it, without taking for granted anything save the existence of mind and ideas, he cannot do so. Let the words that stand for objective realities be supposed to stand for our ideas of them, and the argument becomes meaningless. If it be said that these objective realities are but hypothetically assumed for the purpose of meeting an opponent, it is replied that this cannot be, for Berkeley's reasonings are in truth his justification of Idealism to his own mind; and if he could justify Idealism to his own mind without making these assumptions, he could show us the way. How, then, can his argument be valid? An assumption may be legitimate if the reasoning based on it, by bringing out a result congruous with known truths, prove the assumption true. But what if the reasoning prove the assumption false, whilst the very terms of the reasoning presuppose its truth? We do, indeed, in mathematics assume a certain number to be the answer to a given question, and on this assumption legitimately base an argument which, by ending in an absurdity, disproves the assumption. In such case, however, the successive steps do not become possible only by the truth of the number assumed; for they may be as well gone through with any other number. But if the argument ended in proving that there was no such thing as number, it would do what Berkeley's argument does. It would base upon a thing's existence the proof of its non-existence.

This reasoning in dialogue offers, indeed, great facilities for gaining a victory. When you can put into an adversary's mouth just such replies and admissions as fit your purpose, there is little difficulty in reaching the desired conclusion. Throughout the discussion, Hylas repeatedly assents to things which on his opponent's own principles he should not have assented to. Thus, shortly after the outset, Philonous, with the view of proving the purely subjective character of heat, obtains from Hylas the admission, that an "intense degree of heat is a very great pain." He then asks-"Is your material substance a senseless being, or a being endowed with sense and perception?" to which Hylas replies-"It is senseless, without doubt." "It cannot, therefore, be the subject of pain," continues Philonous. "By no means," rejoins Hylas. And Philonous then goes on to argue, that as an intense heat is a pain, and as a pain cannot exist in a senseless material substance, it follows that an intense heat can exist only in a perceiving mind. But what right has Hylas to make the answers he does? The argument sets out with the position that sensible things are the only things we certainly know; these sensible things are defined as "the things we immediately perceive by the senses;" and Philonous, resolutely ignoring everything else, says:-"Whatever other qualities, therefore, you speak of, as distinct from these, I know nothing of them." Had Hylas, as he should have done, taken the same ground, the dialogue would have run thus:-

Phil. Is material substance a senseless being, or a being endowed with sense and perception?

Hyl. I cannot say.

Phil. How do you mean you cannot say?

Hyl. I mean that, like you, "I know nothing" of any qualities of bodies save those I immediately perceive by the senses; and I cannot immediately perceive by the senses whether material substance is senseless or not.

Phil. But you do not doubt that it is senseless?

Hyl. Yes; in the same way that you doubt my external reality-doubt whether I am anything more than one of your ideas. Did we not, at the beginning, Philonous, distinguish between things known immediately and things known mediately?

Phil. Yes.

Hyl. Did you not make me admit that sensations are the only sensible things; that is, the only things immediately perceived; and that I cannot know the causes of these sensations immediately, but can only know them mediately by reasoning?

Phil. I did.

Hyl. And your whole argument is an attempt to show that these things which I know mediately-these things, whose existence I infer as the causes of my sensations, do not exist at all.

Phil. True.

Hyl. How, then, can you put any trust in my reply, when I either say that matter is sensitive, or that it is not sensitive? The only sensitiveness that I can immediately perceive is my own.

Phil. You know that I am sensitive.

Hyl. Yes, but how? I see you turn when spoken to, and shrink when burned; from such facts, joined with my personal experiences, I infer that you are sensitive as I am; and if you must have an answer to your question, I infer that matter is not sensitive, because it shows no such signs.

Phil. Well.

Hyl. Well! do you not see that if you adopt this answer your whole reasoning is vitiated? You set out to disprove a certain portion of my mediate knowledge. To do this, you now ask from me another portion of my mediate knowledge, as you have already asked several, and will, I suppose, ask more. You are combining these many portions of mediate knowledge, and will draw from them a conclusion; and this conclusion-this piece of doubly mediate knowledge, you will, I suppose, offer to me in place of the mediate knowledge you would disprove. Certainly I shall reject it. I demand that every link in your argument shall consist of immediate knowledge. If but one of them is an inference, and not a thing "immediately perceived by sense," I shall say that your conclusion has the same uncertainty with this that you combat, plus the uncertainty attendant on all argument. Nay, indeed, were every step in your demonstration a piece of immediate knowledge, I should argue that as the inference you drew was but mediate knowledge, it could have no greater warrant than the adverse one. As it is, however, your inference, as judged by your own principles, has incomparably less warrant.

Space permitting, it might be argued at length that Berkeley confounds the having a sensation with the knowledge of having a sensation. Unconsciously doing homage to the principle that the fewer times the Universal Postulate is assumed, the more certain is the conclusion, he professes to recognise that only which is immediately perceived-that which involves but one assumption of the postulate, and declines to recognise the mediate perceptions which involve it more than once. Yet what he starts with as primary and unquestionable facts belong to this last class. Whilst the reception of a sensation may be a simple undecomposable mental act, to observe the reception of a sensation is decidedly a composite one. The knowledge of having a sensation, so far from being an act of immediate consciousness, presupposes a much involved process. It presupposes a synthesis of those ideas constituting the notion of personal identity, and then a recollection of how that personal identity has just been affected. Or, to state the position in another form-It is impossible for any one to know he has a sensation without self-consciousness becoming an element of his thought. Self-consciousness, however, can never be known immediately, but only by recollection. No one can be conscious of what he is, but only of what he was a moment since. That which thinks can never be the object of direct contemplation, seeing that to be this it must become that which is thought of, not that which thinks. It is impossible to be at the same time that which regards and that which is regarded. We never can be literally self-conscious, but can only know at each instant what we were the instant before; and can but infer present existence from the cognition of existence just past. And if self-consciousness cannot be immediate knowledge, nothing can be immediate knowledge into which self-consciousness enters as one concept. Therefore, the knowledge of having sensations cannot be immediate knowledge. Were the consciousness of sensations the same thing as the consciousness of receiving sensations, Berkeley's first step would be unassailable. As it is, however, the assumption on which his whole argument rests, is open to the same criticism that he himself passes on the adverse assumption; namely, that it is not a perception, but a synthesis of perceptions.

But the true answer to Idealism-the answer of which the foregoing must be regarded as adumbrations-is involved in the answer to Scepticism, to which let us now turn.

§ 8. Hume's doubts as to the validity of reason, should have led him not to a state of suspense, but to an entire rejection of all his conclusions. Such a course might be proved logically necessary, even from his own point of view. Let us, however, suppose him to be in possession of the views above advanced, and then observe the course his scepticism must take.

"I doubt whether my subjective beliefs have any objective basis; that is, when I have an impression, I have no proof that there is anything external causing it; that is, though I cannot for a moment rid myself of the belief that there is something, yet there may be nothing. But how do I know that there may be nothing?"

"Reason tells me so."

"But if, when I say-'It is impossible for the same thing to be and not to be,' I say so because I have an invariably existent belief to that effect-a belief proved to invariably exist by my inability to conceive its negation; and if, when I draw a conclusion from this logical aphorism, I do so by saying that if the aphorism be true, I have a similarly indestructible belief that my deduction is true; then it follows that all my reasoning consists in concluding those things to be true in which I have an indestructible belief-a belief proved indestructible by my inability to conceive its negation."

"But I have just this kind of belief in an external world. Now that I am looking at the table, I find that by no effort, however violent, can I conceive that the table is an impression in me and not a thing outside of me. I can make a verbal proposition to that effect, but I am quite incapable of making my thoughts respond to it. Whilst looking away from the table, I can vaguely conceive that the fact might be so; but whilst looking at the table, I feel it utterly impossible to conceive that the fact is so."

"Evidently, then, my conviction that there is an external world has the same warrant as every step in my argument has-is simply arrived at by an argument of one step."

"Hence to conclude that there is no proof of an external world is to reason my way to the conclusion that reason is fallacious. But if reason be fallacious, then the reasoning by which I prove the fallacy of reason is itself fallacious. Then reason is not fallacious. Then its inferences respecting the fallacy of reason are true. And so on perpetually."

"It results, therefore, from my position, that it is impossible to decide whether reason is fallacious or not fallacious."

"Be it which it may, however, it is clear that my scepticism is not logically justifiable. If reason be not fallacious, then is the single-stepped argument which proves the existence of objects, valid. If it be fallacious, then it is manifestly impossible to shake an argument of one step by an argument of many steps."

Leaving general statements of the case, and setting ourselves to consider it fundamentally, we find that the whole question at issue resolves itself into this-Which is the more certain, the existence of objects or the existence of impressions and ideas? Possibly some of the foregoing considerations may have led the reader to suspect that Philosophy has after all given a wrong answer to this question. If so, they will have prepared the way for an examination into the relative validity of our beliefs in subjective and objective things, as tested by the number of times the Universal Postulate is assumed in arriving at each belief respectively. And, to avoid reasoning in a circle, he will see the propriety of sweeping his mind clear of hypotheses, so that, freed from all disturbing influences, it may be brought to bear afresh upon the facts.

Having as far as possible done this, let him contemplate an object-this book, for instance. Resolutely refraining from theorizing, let him now say what he finds. He finds that his consciousness is filled with the existence of the book. Does there enter into this state of his consciousness any notion about sensations? No; he finds that such notion, so far from being contained in his consciousness, has to be fetched from elsewhere, to the manifest disturbance of his then state of consciousness. Does he perceive that the thing he is conscious of is an image of the book? Not at all; so little does his consciousness know of any image, that it is only by remembering his metaphysical readings that he can suppose such image to exist. So long as he refuses to translate the facts into any hypothesis, he feels that he is conscious of the book, and not of an impression of the book-of an objective thing, and not of a subjective thing. He feels that the sole content of his consciousness is the book considered as an external reality. He feels that this recognition of the book as an external reality is a simple indivisible act. Whether originally separable into premises and inference or not (a question which he manifestly cannot here entertain), he feels that this act is undecomposable. And, lastly, he feels that, do what he will, he cannot reverse this act-he cannot, whilst contemplating the book, believe that it is non-existent-he cannot conceive that where he sees it there is nothing. Hence, whilst he continues looking at the book, his belief in it as an external reality possesses the highest validity possible. It has the direct guarantee of the Universal Postulate; and it assumes the Universal Postulate only once.

Possibly he will object that though this belief apparently involves but one assumption of the postulate, it really involves two-that he not only postulates the object, but that in doing so he postulates himself. Doubtless if his thought is-"I know the book exists," he postulates himself as well as the object. But his primary thought is simply-"The book exists;" and his own being is no more postulated in that thought than it is in these words which express it. Sir William Hamilton does indeed assert that we are conscious of subject and object "in the same indivisible moment of intuition;" but as was hinted in passing, this assertion will not be uniformly assented to; and it here becomes needful to assign reasons for dissenting from it.

Under ordinary circumstances, the time during which any one state of consciousness continues uninterrupted is so brief that it is impossible to distinctly identify it. These words, though successively occupying the reader's mind as symbols, are yet so instantaneously followed by their meanings that their symbolism passes unobserved. Moreover, whilst recognising and interpreting them his mind is rapidly taking note of other things-of the paper they are printed on, of his hands, of other parts of his body within view, of the sensations that periodically lead him to change his posture, and of the sounds and movements going on around him. Manifestly were there no other evidence it might, on the one hand, be argued as before, that some of the phenomena thus rapidly succeeding one another must be very liable to be mistaken for simultaneous ones; whilst, on the other hand, it might be reasonably inferred that as the more observable facts of consciousness form a series, so do the less observable ones; and that strictly no two things can be present to consciousness at the same instant, or known "in the same indivisible moment of intuition."

When we turn from ordinary circumstances to extraordinary ones we obtain sufficiently clear indications of the fact that the consciousness of objective existence is accompanied by an unconsciousness of subjective existence. Let the thing perceived be a very astonishing one, and the observer becomes perceptibly oblivious of himself. Our ordinary language recognises this fact. We say of such an one that he is absorbed in contemplation, lost in wonder, has forgotten himself; and we describe him as afterwards returning to himself, recollecting himself. From a deeply interested spectator who is so far possessed by his perception as not to hear what is said to him, up to the stupified victim of an impending catastrophe, may be seen all grades of this state. Under this last and extreme degree of it persons are killed, from the inability to recover their self-consciousness in time to avoid danger. Even those who, in such case, are not completely paralyzed, manifest much the same mental state; for it frequently happens that they are wounded without knowing it, and they are generally surprised to hear afterwards what they did whilst in peril-a fact proving that their actions were automatic rather than conscious. Probably most on being reminded of these truths will be able to recall the perceptible period, during which a startling sight or sound occupies consciousness to the exclusion of the idea of self; and all who do this will see that an ordinary perception as well as an extraordinary one, must, while it lasts, exclude the idea of self, but that it lasts too short a time to admit of the exclusion being observed.

The strongest reason, however, for asserting that the subject is not postulated in perceiving an object, is, that the subject can be known only by regarding itself as an object. All notion of self consists either in the impressions of self received through the senses and in recollections and combinations of them (in which case there can be no notion of self when the first perception is received); or else it is an assumed something by which these impressions andc. are contemplated, but which, as it cannot contemplate itself directly, can know itself only by contemplating its past acts-can know itself only by the objective registry which it has just left of itself. On either hypothesis self can be known only as an object. Hence, to say that consciousness of subject and object is simultaneous is to say that in perceiving one object we necessarily perceive another object; which seems alike a gratuitous and an improbable assumption.

Thus there is good ground for the belief that the cognition of the non-ego does not involve a simultaneous cognition of the ego-ground which is strengthened by the remembrance that we can express cognition of objective being in words that involve no assertion of subjective being (the book exists), which we could not do did the one conception involve the other-and ground yet further strengthened by the consideration that we can perfectly well conceive an object to remain in existence after our own annihilation, which it would be impossible to do if the cognition of subject and object were simultaneous and consequently inseparable. Further inquiry therefore serves to confirm, rather than to shake, the direct verdict of consciousness-that the cognition of an object as an external reality is an undecomposable mental act involving the Universal Postulate once only.

Turn we now to the hypotheses which serve as fulcra for the attempted overthrow of Realism, beginning, as we may properly do, with Hypothetical Realism-the comparatively unassuming one from which the others have sprung, but whose parentage they have in their high pretensions found it convenient to ignore.

No one can form any conception of the representative hypothesis without abandoning his first centre of consciousness, in which he is simply percipient, and taking up another position, from which to inspect the act of percipience. A spectator gazing at a fire is simply conscious of the fire; if you tell him he cannot know the fire, but merely his sensation of a fire, he can realize your meaning only by regarding both the fire and himself as objects, and observing how the one affects the other. What now is involved in this proceeding? He postulates the fire; he postulates himself; and he postulates the relation between these. In his original state of percipience, not only does his cognition of the fire seem immediate and undecomposable, but he cannot even conceive that it may be a compound cognition, without going much out of his way to do so. Whereas in this state to which you bring him, not only does the alleged representative cognition seem at once decomposable into three things, but he cannot even conceive it without the three things. In the one case he cannot by any effort use the postulate more than once; in the other, he cannot by any effort avoid using it three times.

Thus too is it with Absolute Idealism. Idealism assumes that minds are entities, that ideas are entities, and that ideas exist in minds. Even supposing that it has the guarantee of the Universal Postulate for each of these, yet, as involving them all, its proposition has three times the liability to error possessed by the proposition it sets out to disprove. Let it be granted that its belief-mind is an entity, is a belief proved by the inconceivableness of its negation to invariably exist (which is not the fact; for mind is conceivable as not an entity, but a process); let it be granted that it has the like authority for the belief-ideas are entities (which is not the fact; for ideas are conceivable as phases of the process, mind); and let it be granted, that for its belief-ideas exist in mind, it has this same highest warrant (which is not the fact; for it is conceivable that ideas are not in mind but are mind)-let it be granted, we say, that each of these beliefs is indisputable, still, Idealism stands in the position of being unable to frame its hypothesis without thrice making an assumption which the adverse hypothesis makes but once.

At first sight, the scepticism of Hume, by not asserting the existence of mind, escapes this difficulty. But the escape is apparent only. In reality, Hume makes even more assumptions than Berkeley does. He sets out by saying, that our perceptions resolve themselves into impressions and ideas; and on this division all his reasoning hinges. Obviously, did he merely postulate these two things, the foundation of his argument would be less certain than the undecomposable belief he calls in question. But he artfully postulates more than two things, without seeming to do so. For what is contained in the concept-an impression? Translate the word into thought, and there are manifestly involved a thing impressing and a thing impressed. It is impossible to attach any idea to the word save by the help of these other ideas. Without contending at length, as we might, that our conceptions of things impressing and things impressed are gained by seeing bodies act upon each other, and that we cannot realize these conceptions without assuming the objectivity of such bodies-without dwelling upon the illegitimacy of an argument which assumes that there are impressions, and then goes on to show that there are neither things impressing nor things impressed, and which thus taking the abstract for its fulcrum, proposes to overset the concrete from which it is abstracted,-without dwelling upon this, it suffices our present purpose to remark, that unless Hume postulates the three things-the impression, the impressing, and the impressed, his reasoning is meaningless from the very beginning. Unless its constituent words are the signs of thoughts, an argument is a mere game of symbols. Refrain from rendering your terms into ideas, and you may reach any conclusion whatever. The whole is equal to its part, is a proposition that may be quite comfortably entertained so long as neither wholes nor parts are imagined. If, then, Hume's argument claim to be anything more than a string of logical forms containing no substance, its first term-an impression, must be used only as the representative of a definite concept; and no such definite concept can be formed without two other things-the impressing and the impressed-being involved. The existence of ideas being further involved as an essential part of Hume's premises, it results that (saying nothing about the assumed relation between impressions and ideas) he postulates four things to the one thing postulated by Realism.

So that, even did these idealist, sceptical, and other kindred theories require no long chains of syllogisms to get from their premises to conclusions at variance with Realism-were their conclusions immediately, instead of remotely, consequent on the premises-they would still be placed in the dilemma that their respective assumptions are three and four times more liable to error than the assumption they dispute.

As a last resort it will perhaps be urged, that the proposition of Realism is still an inference, and not an intuition-that our notion of the externality of things is not immediate, but involves a synthesis. The first reply is, that we cannot possibly know that our notion of their externality is a synthesis, with anything like the certainty with which we can know that their externality is real. As the reasoning employed to prove the synthetic nature of the realistic belief, is itself a synthesis of a highly complicated kind, whilst the synthesis of Realism is one of the simplest possible-so simple as to have become organic-it follows that any such objection to Realism is, like its many kindred ones, self-destructive; it repeatedly assumes the validity of that whose validity it questions. The second reply is, that all knowledge whatever involves synthesis; and that no metaphysical hypothesis can be framed without a more complex synthesis than that required by Realism. Instance the proposition-Ideas exist in mind. Here are three syntheses. An idea is a general word applicable to any state of consciousness, and, as we see in the child, comes to have a meaning only after the putting together of many experiences. Mind is a synthesis of states of consciousness-is a thing we can form no notion of without re-membering, re-collecting some of our mental acts. Every conception of relation is a synthesis-that of inclusion being one. The child is enabled to recognise one thing as in another, by a series of observations similar to, and simultaneous with, those that teach it the externality of things; and until these observations have been generalized, the proposition that ideas are in minds must be unthinkable. Thus, then, each of the words idea, in, mind, involves a synthesis; and the proposition-Ideas exist in mind, is a synthesis of syntheses. Passing from the assumptions of Idealism to its argument, it might be shown that each of its syllogisms is a synthesis of syntheses; and that its conclusion, reached by putting together many syllogisms, is a synthesis of syntheses of syntheses. Instead, then, of the realistic belief being objectionable on the ground of its synthetic nature, its superiority is, that it is less open to this objection than any other belief which can be framed.

The grossly fallacious character of every metaphysical doctrine at variance with ordinary credence, and of the scepticism which forms the logical outcome common to them all, will, however, from our present stand-point, be most vividly perceived on considering the general aspect and pretension of their arguments, or rather of the sceptical argument regarded as a type of the class. For, granting the sceptic his premises, and making no objection to his reasoning, what is the sum total of his achievement? Simply this; that by a long and involved series of steps he brings Realism's belief in the existence of objects to a reductio ad absurdum. But his conclusion that objects do not exist, Realism brings to a reductio ad absurdum by a single step. At best, then, he does but offer a many-stepped reductio ad absurdum in place of a single-stepped one. What, now, is the worth of such an offer? If the reductio ad absurdum afford valid proof, the belief of Realism is true. If it do not afford valid proof, what becomes of the sceptic's argument? Awkward as this dilemma looks, it will appear worse on remembering that every one of the many syllogisms by which scepticism reaches its goal, tacitly assumes the validity of the reductio ad absurdum. Not only where Hume from time to time says, "For 'tis evident," and "'tis impossible to conceive," andc., but in every successive sentence, in everything he asserts, in everything he denies, he takes for granted the infallibility of the realist's test. He cannot move a single step on the way to his own conclusion, without postulating that which disproves his conclusion.

Scepticism, then, is reducible to this extreme predicament-that the assumption on which it founds its argument is less certain than the assumption it sets out to disprove; that each of the many steps in its argument is less certain (as involving a more complex synthesis) than the single step of the adverse argument; and that it cannot take any one of these many steps without endorsing that adverse argument.

§ 9. It is curious to see a doctrine which positively contradicts our primary inferences chosen as a refuge from another doctrine which simply doubts them. In the philosophy of Kant, however, this is done. Scepticism merely questions all things, and professes to decisively affirm nothing. Kantism, in anxiety to escape it, decisively affirms things contrary to universal belief. That Space and Time are "forms of sensibility" or "subjective conditions of thought" that have no objective basis, is as repugnant to common sense as any proposition that can be framed. And to adopt this proposition instead of the one that we have no sufficient evidence of any objective existence, seems to be a preference of the greater evil to the less.

Of the general criticisms that may be passed upon the hypothesis that Space and Time are conditions or forms of the ego, impressed by it on the non-ego in the act of perception, one is, that it gratuitously entails difficulties to avoid what are not difficulties. For if, in congruity with the ordinary belief, we suppose the non-ego to exist under certain universal conditions or forms, it will obviously follow that in being impressed upon the ego the non-ego must carry its universal conditions or forms along with it, and must generate in the ego corresponding conditions or forms that will be also universal. The facts, therefore, are quite explicable on the supposition that all knowledge is from experience. If, on the other hand, to explain these facts, it be assumed that the conditions belong to the ego, and the materials to the non-ego, it results that the non-ego is unconditioned. But unconditioned existence is inconceivable. Consequently, it becomes impossible to conceive that there can be any non-ego at all. If it be replied that the hypothesis itself involves that we cannot conceive anything without impressing our own forms of thought upon it, and that therefore an unconditioned non-ego is by the hypothesis inconceivable, even though existent, the rejoinder is, that an existence of which we have no evidence, which we cannot conceive, and which it is impossible that we should conceive, is an existence we have as strong a warrant for denying as we have for denying anything.

On turning from the abstract to the concrete, this gratuitous making of difficulties is still more clearly seen. The fact on which Kant bases his assertion, that Space is a subjective form and not an objective reality-the fact, namely, that we can conceive the annihilation of bodies, but cannot conceive the annihilation of space-is a fact quite comprehensible on the hypothesis that all knowledge is from without. We know Space simply as an ability to contain things. Whatever other idea of it we seem to have is nothing more than a synthesis of our experiences of this ability; and may be decomposed into such experiences. We can form no notion of Space without imagining dimensions. Our conceptions of it are made by abstracting from bodies their lengths and breadths, and putting these together by themselves in a more or less distinct way; and evidently the conceptions thus formed can be essentially nothing but conceptions of an ability to contain bodies having such lengths and breadths. The further conceptions we gain by the focal adjustments of the eyes, and by the motions of the body and limbs, are manifestly built upon this; and when analyzed yield nothing more than this. If, then, we know Space simply as an ability to contain things, the fact that we cannot conceive its annihilation, is quite accountable on the experience-hypothesis. Bodies we can conceive annihilated, because by evaporation, and by burning, we have seen them annihilated-annihilated, that is, to the senses. But the ability to contain bodies we cannot conceive annihilated because we have never known it absent. In all our experience that ability has remained constant; and hence the conception of it is similarly constant in our minds. Evidently, then, our powerlessness to conceive the non-existence of Space requires no such hypothesis as that of Kant for its explanation. And we are, therefore, not obliged to take to the anomaly which that hypothesis presents; namely, that though Space is a property of the ego, yet we cannot conceive it to disappear when the ego disappears.

Were it only that the experience-hypothesis explains all that the Kantian hypothesis is invented to explain, and does this without involving us in such insurmountable difficulties, its superiority would be sufficiently marked. But it does more. It accounts for a certain peculiarity in our conceptions of Space, which the Kantian hypothesis does not account for; this peculiarity being, that every conception of Space which can be formed by a single mental act is limited to such portion of Space as we can have experience of at one time. Let any one attempt to form an idea of the whole surrounding sphere of Space simultaneously, and he will find it impossible to do so. When standing upright, he can very well conceive the hemisphere of Space extending in front of him; but he cannot in the same act of thought include the hemisphere of Space that is behind. On watching his mind, he will perceive that to think of the Space that is behind, he must become unconscious of the Space that is in front. If to get rid of all perturbing circumstances, he mentally abolishes the Earth and all objects, and supposes himself in an infinite void, he will still find that the infinity at any moment occupying his imagination is the infinity extending on one side of him, and never the infinity on both sides. Now the Kantian hypothesis not only leaves this fact unaccounted for, but is at variance with it; for if Space be a form of thought, our conception of it should be simple, total, uniform, and altogether unrelated to external perception. Whereas, the experience hypothesis not only accounts for it, but involves it, as an inevitable deduction; for if all knowledge is from without, the conception which we can by one act form of Space cannot exceed the perception which one act can give us of it. To the first theory the fact is an obstacle: to the second it is a confirmation.

Passing from these general criticisms to the fundamental criticism, the first thing to be noticed is, that Kant does involuntary homage to the Universal Postulate in assigning grounds for his dogma. Not to dwell upon the fact that his whole argument turns upon the existence of Space and Time, and that for the belief in their existence the Universal Postulate is his sole warrant; and only observing, by the way, that the distinction he draws between these and other things, hinges entirely upon conceivableness and inconceivableness, we go on to remark, that he infers from our inability to conceive the annihilation of Space and Time, conjoined with our ability to conceive the annihilation of all other things-he infers from these facts, that Space and Time are receptivities, subjective conditions and not objective realities. We can conceive bodies non-existent: we cannot conceive Time and Space non-existent: therefore, Time and Space are forms of thought.

What now is the worth of his "therefore"? At the best merely this; that given these premises, there arises an indestructible belief in this conclusion. Our conceptions of Time and Space comporting themselves thus, the inference that they are subjective follows as a belief proved by the inconceivableness of its negation to invariably exist. Only reminding the reader that, as above shown, it does not thus follow; it is here to be observed, that, granting his whole position, Kant has no higher guarantee for his inference than the Universal Postulate. The thing must be so, he says; and the entire meaning of this "must" is, that no other thing can be conceived.

Having by implication assumed the validity of this canon of belief, whose warrant he wrongly supposes himself to have, what does Kant do? He forthwith asserts that which this canon denies, and denies that which this canon asserts. The subjectivity of Time and Space being, he alleges, irresistible as an inference, he insists on it as a fact; and to receive it as a fact involves two impossibilities-the forming of concepts of Time and Space as subjective forms, and the abolition of the concepts of Time and Space as objective realities. The truth is, that Kant's proposition is both positively unthinkable in itself, and immediately involves a positively unthinkable consequence.

Consider, first, the thing affirmed-that Time and Space are subjective conditions of thought, or properties of the ego. Is it possible to construct any concept answering to these words? or are they not simply groups of signs which seem to contain a notion, but which really contain none? An attempt to construct the notion will quickly show that the last is the fact. Think of Space-of the thing, that is; not of the word. Now think of self-of that which is conscious. And then, having clearly realized these concepts, put the two together, and conceive the one as a property of the other. What results? Nothing but a conflict of two thoughts that cannot be united. It would be as practicable to imagine a round square. What, then, is the worth of the proposition? As Mr. Mansel, himself a Kantist, says in his "Prolegomena Logica:"-

"A form of words uniting attributes not presentable in an intuition, is not the sign of a thought, but of the negation of all thinking. Conception must thus be carefully distinguished, as well from mere imagination, as from a mere understanding of the meaning of words. Combinations of attributes logically impossible may be expressed in language perfectly intelligible. There is no difficulty in understanding the meaning of the phrase bilinear figure, or iron-gold. The language is intelligible, though the object is inconceivable."

If this be true, Kant's proposition is empty sound. If, as Sir William Hamilton says, those propositions only are conceivable of which subject and predicate are capable of unity of representation, then is the subjectivity of Space inconceivable; for it is impossible to bring the two notions, Space and property of ego, into unity of representation.

Such being the character of the proposition affirmed, consider now the character of the proposition which is, by implication, denied; viz., that Time and Space are objective realities. The negation of this proposition is as inconceivable as the affirmation of the other. Neither Kant nor any one else ever rid himself of the belief in the externality of Space. That conception of it which he describes as incapable of annihilation is the conception of it as an external non-ego; and if this non-annihilability of the conception be appealed to as having any significance at all, it signifies the validity of the conception in its totality. In short, the belief in Space as an objective reality is a belief proved by the inconceivableness of its negation to invariably exist; and is, therefore, a belief having the highest possible certitude. And the same is manifestly true of Time.

See then the position in which Kant stands. He assumes, that from our inability to annihilate Space and Time in thought, the inference that they are subjective necessarily follows-follows as an inference, whose negation is inconceivable. But the inference that they are subjective involves two inconceivable things. Kant's proceeding, then, is essentially an assertion of two inconceivabilities in place of one. Recognising by implication the Universal Postulate, he, out of professed submission to its authority, straightway twice denies its authority. He chooses a double impossibility to escape from a single one. Granting his assumption, therefore, his proposition is indefensible; and when his assumption proves to be unwarrantable-when, as we have seen, the inference which he thinks necessary, turns out to be not necessary-the accumulated absurdity of his position becomes strikingly apparent.

The systems of Fichte, Schelling, and Hegel, are manifestly open to parallel criticisms-criticisms, however, which, as being substantially repetitions of the foregoing, it is needless here to detail.

§ 10. Do we not thus, then, reach the desired reconciliation between Philosophy and Common Sense? We have seen, first, that the existence of beliefs is, in so far as our reasoning faculties are concerned, the fundamental fact; next, that beliefs which invariably exist are those which, both logically and of necessity, we must adopt; further, that those are invariably existent beliefs, of which we cannot conceive the negations; and lastly, that whether beliefs having this warrant be infallible or not, it must equally happen that the fewer times we assume the validity of such warrant in reaching any conclusion, the more certain must that conclusion be. These positions being granted, it inevitably results, as we have found, that the current belief in objects as external independent entities, has a higher guarantee than any other belief whatever-that our cognition of existence considered as noumenal has a certainty which no cognition of existence, considered as phenomenal, can ever approach; or, in other words-that, judged logically as well as instinctively, Realism is the only rational creed; and that all adverse creeds are self-destructive.

From our present point of view, not only does the seeming discordance between the verdicts of abstract and practical reason wholly disappear, but their verdicts explain each other. On the one hand, the extreme vividness and unconquerable strength of our common-sense convictions correspond with the extreme brevity of the process by which each of them is arrived at; or, in other words-with the single assumption of the Universal Postulate which each of them involves. On the other hand, the shadowy and unconvincing character of metaphysical inferences corresponds with the extreme complexity of the arguments by which they are drawn; that is-with the numerous assumptions of the Universal Postulate they severally imply. Thus our involuntary adhesion to the first, and our inability to hold the last, answer to their respective claims as measured by the fundamental test of credibility. The instinct justifies the logic: the logic accounts for the instinct. It was hinted at the outset, that an inquiry into our knowledge by means of our knowledge must, if rightly conducted, be consistent in its results-that the analysis of Philosophy must agree with the synthesis of Common Sense. This we now find to be the fact; not simply as shown in the coincidence of their conclusions, but as further shown in the rationale afforded by the one of the confidence felt by the other.

Here, too, we may remark the identity of the illusion common to all metaphysical reasonings; the illusion, namely, that our cognition of logical necessity has a higher certainty than our cognition of anything else. Not recognising the fact, that for the validity of every step in an argument, we have no better guarantee than we have for an intuition of sense, but assuming, on the contrary, that whilst our simple perceptions of external existences are fallible, our complex perceptions of internal co-existences are infallible-assuming this, men have sought to reach by reasoning a knowledge that transcends ordinary knowledge. That it is possible by a chain of syllogisms to gain a conviction more positive than any conviction immediately derived from the senses, is the assumption which every metaphysical argument tacitly makes. The endeavour by one school to establish an Ontology, and the assertion by another, that we cannot prove the existence of noumena, alike take for granted that demonstration has a validity exceeding that of intuition. To Common Sense, standing steadfastly on a given spot, the first says that there is a series of steps by which that spot may be arrived at; the second says that there is no such series; but they agree in saying, that until a series of steps has been gone through, Common Sense cannot stand on that spot at all. This superstition in mental dynamics has a curious analogy to a current superstition in physical dynamics. Much as the mechanic, familiar with the effects of levers, wheels, and pulleys, has come to attribute to them intrinsic powers, the metaphysician, struck with the results achieved through logical forms, ascribes a virtue to the forms themselves; and as the one hopes by an arrangement of these levers, wheels, and pulleys, to generate force, so does the other hope by some logical combination to evolve certainty. In both cases, however, the result is directly the reverse. As every additional part of a mechanical apparatus entails a loss of force, so does every syllogism entail a loss of certainty. As no machine can produce an effect equivalent to the moving power, so no argument can establish a conclusion equally certain with that primary knowledge from which all argument is derived.

It remains but to notice Scepticism's last refuge; namely, the position that we can never truly know that things are as they seem; and that whilst it may be impossible for us to think of them as otherwise, yet they may be otherwise. This position we shall find to be as logically inadmissible as it is practically unthinkable. For one of two things must be true of it: it must either admit of no justification by reason, or it must admit of some justification. If it admits of no justification by reason, then it amounts to a tacit negation of all reason. It posits that as possible which by its own admission can be entertained not as a conceivable proposition, but only as a verbally intelligible one; and if it be allowable, without assigning grounds, to do this in the present case, it is allowable to do it in any case; whence it will follow that every conclusion can be met by a counter conclusion which may be posited as possible; and all conclusions being thus rendered worthless, intelligence is abolished. If, on the other hand, reasons in justification of the position be assigned-if it be alleged that we cannot know that things are as they seem because we cannot transcend consciousness-then there is at once taken for granted the validity of that test whose validity is called in question. The Universal Postulate is assumed and denied in the same breath. As it has been more than once shown, the invariably existent belief, which is our warrant for asserting the reality of Matter, Space, and Time, is likewise our warrant, and our sole warrant, for every because; and to assume the trustworthiness of this warrant in the one case for the purpose of proving its untrustworthiness in the other, is the climax of absurdity. Evidently, then, we cannot rationally entertain a thought at variance with these primary dicta of consciousness. It is impossible for us to take a single step towards invalidating them without committing a logical suicide.

Footnote

1. The reader must be warned against the confusion that may arise from the double sense in which the word belief is commonly employed, and in which we, too, have been obliged to employ it. Men habitually express a belief in a thing, and at other times they call the thing believed, a belief. We have given

the word two parallel meanings; using it in the one case to describe the persistence of a state of consciousness, and in the other a persistent state of consciousness. The context will, in each case, show in which sense it is to be understood.

www.ingramcontent.com/pod-product-compliance
Lightning Source LLC
Chambersburg PA
CBHW060344290526
45791CB00004B/1524